OSCAR J

"Skipper Can no Longer Play . . ."
and "Daddy Can no Longer Stay . . ."

Sherlene Adolphe

authorHOUSE®

AuthorHouse™ UK Ltd.
1663 Liberty Drive
Bloomington, IN 47403 USA
www.authorhouse.co.uk
Phone: 0800.197.4150

Published by AuthorHouse   11/19/2013

ISBN: 978-1-4918-7992-4 (sc)
ISBN: 978-1-4918-7993-1 (e)

OSCAR J

"Skipper Can no Longer Play . . ."

Dedication

To our Good Lord in Heaven above.

And to my wonderful mother Felixa for her unconditional love.

Acknowledgements

All those who provided me with support and assistance know who they are, but in no particular order a huge thank you to;

My Aunt Ureta, and her daughter—my cousin Sujan, who were the driving forces to get me to focus once again on my dream.

To Uncle John for his encouragement in my putting pen to paper, and to his daughter—my cousin Amanda, for her assistance along the way.

To Pernella my younger sis, who through my most difficult times has been nothing but a rock of support to me.

And to my great friend Dentaa, for her constant smooth voice of encouragement.

Introduction

The first in a series of planned publications, Sherlene decided to put pen to paper to bring an awareness to children and young people, of negative future life experiences that may unfortunately befall them.

Written in fictional verse, these short stories were prepared to give all readers an understanding of what *may* be. Thus preparing any child or young person of the same, passing on the valuable messages of how to deal with, and a realisation, that no matter how negative a situation may be, there can be a positive outcome from all!

OSCAR J

"Skipper Can no Longer Play . . ."

For as long as he could remember,
Oscar J had his bouncy dog Skipper with him every day.

For as long as he could remember,
Oscar J and his bouncy dog Skipper would go out to play.

Skipper?

He was a great big dog,
Black and tan,
With huge big paws the size of a grown man's hands.

He'd wag his long tail,
And pant and bark,
As he'd run through the house,
And play fetch in the park.

Every birthday of Oscar's Skipper was there,
Bounding among presents,
Playing musical chairs.

Spring chasing bunnies through the meadow,
Summer catching a Frisbee by the sea,
Autumn running through the bracken,
Christmas lounging beside the tree.

For as long as he could remember . . .

Throughout his nursery,
Infant and now junior school years,
At the end of each long day,
Skip was there to greet Oscar by the front door,
Eagerly waiting to have fun and play.

Then over time Skip could no longer jump as high,
Or even run as fast.
In races where he would have been guaranteed first place,
Now he would almost come last.

With each passing year Skip's fur peppered with grey,
His jet black whiskers began to turn white.
Pain soon came into his joints causing a slight limp,
Followed by some gradual loss of his sight.

"It's all due to old age" said the Vet
"These are problems we would expect,

All I can do is prescribe some medicine for his pain,
The rest we must accept."

"Old age?" Gasped Oscar, "but mum Skip is only thirteen!"
"In doggie years he's over eighty" said Mrs J,
"Older than your Great Nana Pauline."

Where Skip would have preferred to run he could now
only walk,
Where he would have preferred to stand he would now
sit or lay,
Although he'd still eagerly await Oscar's return home
from school,
Skipper would now be too tired to play.

So Oscar would sit with his furry friend,
To scratch behind his ears, beneath his chin, stroke his
tum.
Being fed any treats Oscar found in the cupboard after
school,
Enjoying this quiet time together now as their fun.

Then one day Oscar returned home Skip just wasn't
there.
Not hiding behind any door that he searched or beneath
any chair.
When Oscar called out for Skipper he just didn't come.
Confused—Oscar went in search of his mum.

He found Mrs J in her bedroom.

"Oh Oscar dear, I didn't hear you come in."

"Hi Mum," he then asked; "where's Skip?"

"I have some very sad news I'm afraid, so please come
and take a seat.
As you know Skip was of a grand old age, not as fit as
he used to be,
He had awful pain in his joints, was deaf in one ear and
in the end he could hardly see."

"The end?" Wondered Oscar . . .

"Well my son, it all became too much, and now dear
Skip is no more,
When I arrived from shopping earlier today I found
him laying dead . . .
He'd died by the front door."

"Died?" Repeated Oscar wide eyed.

"Yes. Oh honey I'm ever *so* sorry he's gone!
But now dad's put him in the hands of our local
Veterinary Surgeon."

"Gone!" Repeated a wide eyed Oscar,
"Was it my fault? What did I do?

Did he go because I behaved badly the other day and refused to listen to you?"

"No!" Assured Mrs J

"Well if I'm especially good will he come back?
I promise to now always listen,
Eat my greens, and never again torment our new neighbour's cat!"

"Oscar dear, now that our lovely Skipper has died,
He can no longer breathe, move, hear, or see,
So never again will he be able to come back to;
You, daddy or me."

"What!?"

"Try to imagine Skip's death as though he's in a very, very, deep sleep,
Never to awake from the land of his dreams,
Counting up all of those sheep."

As hard as he tried Oscar J couldn't imagine a life without Skip,
For each part of his life that he could recall Skip had always been in it.

For as long as he could remember . . .

With a huge ache in his heart,
And a pounding head,
Eyes burning with tears Oscar took to mums bed.

Staring through the bedroom window,
Looking up at the cloudy sky,
Tears now rolling down his cheeks Oscar turned to ask
mum; "Why?"

She replied;

"Just as each year green leaves age,
Turn brown and fall dead from a tree,
All that is now living one day will die,
And to lose one that we have cared for and loved,
We may feel the sadness of this loss and may cry."

She stroked his head.

"Now death is not just due to old age,
As Skip's has now come to be,
A severe illness or bad accident,
May cause this to others unfortunately."

"But it's not fair!" Oscar shouted,
"Our new neighbours still have their cat!
Why didn't Julie's two guinea pigs lay down and die?
Or even Daniel's ugly pet rat?"

"Honey this is something called grief that you are feeling,
That only time will heal,
But with each good memory that you can muster,
The less anger and pain you will feel."

"Good memories?" Asked Oscar,
What if I can't remember? What if I forget?"

And with that Mrs J held him tightly as they both wept.

She then soothed . . .

"Honey we have all his belongings,
Films and photos taken throughout the years.
We can put them somewhere special as keepsake,
And perhaps wipe away some of our tears."

Oscar moaned; "it's not fair.
Now my life just wont be the same.
I can't believe die and dead made my best friend
disappear,
Who I will never seen again."

Mrs J replied; "there maybe times when our hurt seems
too much,
Skip is already so dearly missed,
But remember the pain of your grief wont always be so bad,
Especially when you remember to do this . . .

Close your eyes Oscar,
Shut them real tight,
Now imagine the good times with our Skip with all
your might."

"Why?"

"Just try to imagine the sound of his bark,
The feel of his hair . . ."

"It's called fur mum"

"Okay! But do you see him there?"

"Umm?" Oscar wiped his nose.

"Yes I can see him . . . Chasing his ball through the
park,
Wagging his tail by the front door,
Trying to bury a bone out back,
Now he's rolling around on the floor . . .

Now I can hear him!
Snoring at night,
Barking when the postman delivers our mail,"

Oscar giggled and sniffed,
"I can see him begging for scraps in the kitchen,
And now he's chasing his tail!"

Oscar's eyes slowly opened.

"Wow mum! I understand now!
Now I can see!
That even though Skip has gone from our lives,
there **is** a way I can keep him with me!"

*Although the ones we have loved and lost
can never return to us once they have gone,
As long as their memories remain in our minds and
hearts their spirit will forever live on.*

For as long as we can remember . . .

Definitions

In alphabetical order is a list of many words from the story you have just read. Are some completely new to you? Or are there words that you have read or heard of before, but you have just never been sure of what they may mean?

Well no need to pick up a dictionary if you would like to know. As the;

Definitions of each = *Meanings of each*

Are shown here for you below!

Bracken	=	*a plant with leaves that grows on hills and in forests*
Dead / Death	=	*no longer alive*
Die / Died	=	*to stop being alive*
Eagerly	=	*very keen to do something*
Embrace	=	*to put arms around someone to show friendship or love*
Frisbee	=	*a round piece of plastic that is thrown to another in a game outside*

Gradual	=	*a change that may happen slowly and in small amounts*
Grief	=	*a strong feeling of sadness, usually when someone dies*
Guaranteed	=	*you will definitely have it or get it*
Joints	=	*parts of the body that can bend and where two bones meet. Dogs have four joints in each leg*
Limp	=	*to walk in uneven steps because of hurt legs or feet*
Love	=	*a strong feeling of affection when you like someone very much*
Meadow	=	*a field where grass and wild flowers grow*
Memory	=	*something that you remember*
Preferred	=	*when one thing is liked more than another*
Prescribe	=	*a doctor or vet says what type of medicine is needed, and gives a piece of paper that shows it*
Spirit	=	*the part of a person or animal that many people believe, continues to exist after death*
Tum	=	*stomach*
Veterinary Surgeon / Vet	=	*animal Doctor*
Wept	=	*to have cried*

The expression;

'*...**doggie years**...*' = *1 human year is equal to many more years in the life of a dog depending on its size and breed.*

—

Thank you for allowing this book to teach you something new about life!

I hope you have enjoyed!

OSCAR J

"Daddy Can no Longer Stay . . ."

Dedication

To Omar, my beautiful, intelligent, wonderful son!

For all his joy and glory—a true blessing to me his mum!

Acknowledgements

A big thank you for the strength of my faith through the UCKG, and to my Aunt Lena for all I've gained from her Holistic therapies!

Introduction

The first in a series of planned publications, Sherlene decided to put pen to paper to bring an awareness to children and young people, of negative future life experiences that may unfortunately befall them.

Written in fictional verse, these short stories were prepared to give all readers an understanding of what *may* be. Thus preparing any child or young person of the same, passing on the valuable messages of how to deal with, and a realisation, that no matter how negative a situation may be, there can be a positive outcome from all!

OSCAR J

"Daddy can no longer stay . . ."

"Oh just shut up! Just get out!"
Oscar's mum shouted from the hallway below.
"Why don't you just get out of my hair,
Pack up your things and go?"

"You wish it was so simple!" Shouted back his dad
"You're crazy to think I'd just walk away from all I've
ever had!"

Oscar J let out a sob,
Pulling his duvet over his head.
Praying that it would muffle any more that they
shouted.

Tomorrow was the class spelling test,
But with so many words for him to recite,

Oscar couldn't ask mum or dad to help him revise—
they were having *another* fight . . .

**These constant rows had been happening for so many
weeks they seemed like years!
Always involving harsh words, slammed doors, and
many many tears.**

Romantic meals and dances used to be his parents
quality time alone,
When Oscar would get spoilt over at Nanny and Gramps,
Or have fun with the sitter at home.

To the fairground,
Cinemas,
Swimming and to the park,
They went as a family,
And sometimes invited Joseph and his parents from No.23.

Oscar would think back to those times,
When his parents would hug, kiss, and have fun.
Those were of the 'good old days' when Mr J was
besotted with mum!

Now he'd always find mum tearful,
In her bedroom or on the phone,
Telling friends and family what else had gone wrong at
home.

Dad?

He may not be seen now for many days on end.
With mum saying;
"Your dad's away on business."
Or that; "He's staying with a friend."

Dinner at home was no longer fresh and fancy as it used
to be.
It was mainly frozen meals,
Takeaways,
Or pies donated from No.23.

When Aunty Pearl last came to visit she said;
"Sis, you really look a state!"
Mum had swollen eyes from all of her crying,
And was now ill and underweight.

Aunty Pearl advised Mrs J to be honest,
And to no longer pretend.
So that she and Mr J could make a final decision to
bring their awful situation to an end . . .

—

**The kids rushed out as the school bell rang to signal
first play!
Mr Hall approached Oscar,**

Who was again unusually last to leave,
And asked him to wait as he had something to say . . .

"Oscar J I have to ask what has got into you?
You used to be a fine captain of your team and a perfect
prefect at this school.
Now you're always late to class,
Your attendance has become poor,
Your a/b grades are failing—something that's never
happened before.

Do you want to tell me about why you think this is?
It's not just me that's noticed a big change,
But also some of the other kids."

"Why don't they just mind their own business!?"
Shouted Oscar,
"What's it got to do with them?
I bet I know who grassed me up,
And they try to say that they're my friends!"

Oscar looked down at his boots—he had nothing else to
say,
He'd find out who'd spoke his business to Mr Hall and
they were going to pay!

Feeling two hands on his shoulders,
Oscar J looked up,
Mr Hall's eyes were now level with his own,

"Oscar," spoke his teacher with a deep gentle voice,
"Is everything okay at home?"

Hot tears stung the back of Oscar's eyes but now he
didn't care,
It was then his legs seemed to give way and he sunk into
a chair,

Mr Hall grabbed a box of tissues from his desk . . .

—

"I wonder what it's like not to have a dad." Said Ronnie
"Yeah," agreed Susie; "but is Mr J's leaving true?"
"Actually I heard it's Oscar's ma that will get booted
out!" Chuckled Aaron,
"I wonder what *she* was up to?"

"What are you lot saying about my parents?" Shouted
Oscar approaching,
"Aaron how dare you disrespect my mum! You want a
reason to gossip about me and mine? Come here you're
gonna get one!"

Seeing red Oscar swung a punch which would have hit
Aaron square on the chin,
If it wasn't for caretaker Mr Dempsey passing and
quickly jumping in-between . . .

"Sorry sir" Oscar mumbled for the thump he'd now
given Mr Dempsey's chest,
"It's time you followed me to your Head Teacher's office
and lay your fist down for a rest."

Oscar let the school care taker lead the way.

—

Having received an earlier school office call,
Mrs J hurried over the grounds to her son and Mr Hall.

"Mrs J now that you've arrived may we have our word?
I have some bad news about Oscar in a fight I'm afraid."

"A fight?"

"I know, for him it seems completely absurd."

While Oscar was directed to one of the homework
groups in the lower school gym,
Mr Hall proceeded with mum back to his class where
they would both discuss him within.

Oscar hung his head in shame,
Staring at the wooden gym floor,
He couldn't understand why he kept behaving so bad,
He'd never been this way before.

—

Mrs J stared in disbelief,
As she had no idea,
That the problems of the past four or five months,
Had caused Oscar so much despair . . .

Okay he'd wet the bed a few times,
And on weekends he no longer wanted to go out to
play,
But she'd thought this was just a pre-teen phase that
would simply go away.
Sitting there with Mr Hall at 10 minutes past four,
It dawned on Mrs J this supposed phase had been
caused by so very much more . . .

Mrs J apologised,
For although ashamed and embarrassed she did accept,
That Mr Hall's concerns about the 'home life' theory of
her son,
As being totally correct.

When she went to collect Oscar from his group in the
lower school gym,
She vowed never again to lose sight of the most
important person of all—him . . .

—

Much later that evening . . .

In the doorway of his bedroom appeared Oscar's dad.
"Uh oh," worried Oscar,
"He's gonna be so mad."

"Hi Son. Mum phoned me about school today,
And I've decided this madness cannot continue—no way."

"But!" Oscar began,
And then stopped as soon as Mr Jay raised one hand.

"No, this is to be dealt with by both me and mum.
So pop on your slippers and come down,
So we can speak with you son."

Following his dad down the stairs Oscar felt ashamed.
Thinking that he was the cause of all the rows,
Thinking he was the one to blame.

In the lounge,
His parents were at opposite sofa ends for the chat.
Oscar hurried to sit on the floor,
Beside Skippers old toys and mat.
Mrs Jay began . . .

"Once upon a time dad and I were so very happy,
Sadly that has now changed.
Although we still care deeply for one another,
Our lives are no longer the same.

That is why we have decided to divorce,
To part,
To lead our own separate lives,
It's not what either of us ever wanted but staying
together has already been tried."

"Is this my fault?" Cried Oscar,
"What did or didn't I do?"

"Son," Answered Mr J,
"Absolutely none of this has been caused by you!
It's due to my differences with mummy and you're
certainly not to blame,
But so many children think they are the reason for such
'splits',
So I understand why unfortunately you feel the same.
No son. The fault is definitely not your own."

Mrs J then took Oscar's hand.

"Honey this break-up will be a heartache to us all,
Especially poor you,
And for you not to feel any of our sadness and pain is
what we had hoped to do.

Oscar dear from our hearts please accept this apology,
For the pain and disruption that is already in your life,
caused by your daddy and by me."

Oscar nodded his head, looking across at Mr J he then asked;

"Mummy now that daddy is going,
Does it mean you will go too?
If I don't have a mummy or dad then what will I do?
As I'm not near old enough to try and live alone,
Will I get taken by the social and put into a home?"

"Goodness no!" Exclaimed Mr J,
"You'll have two homes—just you wait and see!
One right here with mummy,
And one home away with me.

Christmas and Birthdays will be as special as before,
But now you'll get **not one but two sets of our presents!**
Just a teeny weeny bit more!

"So," asked Oscar, "does this mean you both still love me and want me as your son?"
"Oscar my champ" replied Mr J "that fact has ***never*** been in question!"

Mr J then dropped to his knees,
To kiss Oscar's head,
And to give him a loving tight squeeze!

Oscar's dad then went on to say;

"One thing you can be sure of is that on the day of your birth,
Was the day your mother and I became the proudest parents on earth!"

Sadly in life there may come a time two parents can no longer live as one.
Although a huge change one thing certain to remain is their constant love for their daughters and sons!

Definitions

In alphabetical order is a list of many words from the story you have just read. Are some completely new to you? Or are there words that you have read or heard of before, but you have just never been sure of what they may mean?

Well no need to pick up a dictionary regarding the ones you may not know, as the

Definitions of each = _Meanings of each_

Are shown here for you below!

Absurd	=	_completely stupid or impossible to believe_
Ashamed	=	_feeling guilty and sorry_
Besotted	=	_a strong feeling you have when you like someone very much_
Despair	=	_the feeling that something is so bad nothing can be done to change it_
Disbelief	=	_the feeling of not believing something especially if its shocking or unexpected_

Disrespect	=	*not to show respect to another and hurt their feelings*
Disruption	=	*a disturbance or problem which interrupts an event or activity*
Divorce	=	*when two people end their marriage*
Donated	=	*something given as a gift*
Embarrassed	=	*worried about what others may think*
Harsh	=	*unpleasant and unkind*
Love	=	*a strong feeling of affection when you like someone very much*
Muffle	=	*a sound that is not clear and hard to hear*
Prefect	=	*an older pupil who does special duties and helps teachers with younger pupils*
Pre-teen	=	*children between 9-12 years old*
Proudest	=	*you are so pleased with something and think that its the best*
Recite	=	*say something out loud from memory*
Revise	=	*learn something again to remember for a test*
Row	=	*a noisy, angry, argument*
Separate	=	*when two people separate they go away from each other so that they are no longer together*
Sitter	=	**a** *babysitter*
Sob	=	*a noisy cry*
Theory	=	*an idea about why something happens*

Vowing / Vow   =   *a serious promise*

The expressions;

'... break up ...' &

'... splits ...'   = *when two people end their relationship*

'... dawned on ...' = *when someone begins to realise something and understand*

'... grassed up ...' = *telling someone in authority what someone else has done*

'... quality time ...' = *giving someone your full complete attention*

—

Thank you for allowing this book to teach you something new about life!

I hope you have enjoyed!

About the Author

Born in London England on 6th January 1980, Sherlene Adolphe was raised in Southfields Wimbledon, a London Borough of the same.

Her love for poetry developed from a very early age, and was a regular pastime much to the benefit of her family and friends!

Qualified at Carshalton College in the London Borough of Sutton, Sherlene pursued a successful career in Business Travel, moving on into Lettings and Property Management, all of which she thoroughly enjoyed and excelled.

From the age of twenty one, alongside her formal careers, it was Sherlene's work among children and adolescents within the Social Care sector, that provided her with a great basis of her knowledge and experience of the same. Also a registered Foster Carer, Sherlene currently lives in Beddington village. A tiny rural suburb in Surrey Greater London, with Omar her son.